No Sugar
Low Carb
No Guilt

Japanese-style Desserts

HISAE SAKAMOTO

Marshall Cavendish
Cuisine

Sous Chef: Natsumi Maki
Assistant to Hisae Sakamoto: Junko Burton
Photographer: Tetsuyuki Yamada
Photo Director: Hal Suzuki (Planet Ads and Design P/L, Singapore)
Props: Sinless Lab Food Design, Kyoto
Cover Model: Keira Elizabeth Steele

First published in Japanese by Shuwa System Co., Ltd, 2018

This English edition © 2018 Marshall Cavendish International (Asia) Private Limited

Published by Marshall Cavendish Cuisine
An imprint of Marshall Cavendish International

A member of the
Times Publishing Group

Other Marshall Cavendish Offices:
Marshall Cavendish Corporation. 99 White Plains Road, Tarrytown NY 10591-9001,
USA • Marshall Cavendish International (Thailand) Co Ltd. 253 Asoke, 12th Flr,
Sukhumvit 21 Road, Klongtoey Nua, Wattana, Bangkok 10110, Thailand • Marshall
Cavendish (Malaysia) Sdn Bhd, Times Subang, Lot 46, Subang Hi-Tech Industrial Park,
Batu Tiga, 40000 Shah Alam, Selangor Darul Ehsan, Malaysia.

Marshall Cavendish is a registered trademark of Times Publishing Limited

National Library Board, Singapore Cataloguing-in-Publication Data

Name(s): Sakamoto, Hisae. | Yamada, Tetsuyuki, photographer.
Title: No sugar, low carb, no guilt Japanese-style desserts / Hisae Sakamoto ;
photographer, Tetsuyuki Yamada.
Description: Singapore : Marshall Cavendish Cuisine, [2018] | Previously published: Shuwa
System Co., Ltd, 2018.
Identifier(s): OCN 1048892265 | ISBN 978-981-48-2850-5 (paperback)
Subject(s): LCSH: Desserts. | Sugar-free diet. | Low-carbohydrate diet. | LCGFT: Cookbooks.
Classification: DDC 641.86--dc23

Printed in Singapore

Contents

Introduction

Ten years ago, a friend of mine was diagnosed with diabetes.

Realising that the medication prescribed by the doctors only delayed the progress of diabetes, my friend researched fervently on ways to treat his illness. He found a simple solution: reducing his sugar intake. This meant cutting out table sugar and not eating carbohydrates like white rice and refined wheat products like pasta, noodles and white bread. Coupling this change in diet with conscientious monitoring of his blood sugar level and exercise, my friend found his high blood sugar level returning to normal within two months. A year and a half later, his blood sugar level hardly resembled that of a diabetic person.

While my friend's experience may suggest that sugar is bad for our health, that's not quite true. Our bodies require glucose (a simple sugar) for energy. Our brains need glucose to function. What is bad for health is the consumption of too much sugar. Eating too much carbohydrates (complex sugars which the body breaks down into glucose) can lead to high blood sugar and other negative health problems such as diabetes.

Yet, it is difficult to avoid sugar in our food. Sugar exists in a lot of the food we eat, even vegetables. However, complex sugars being a large part of the human diet is a fairly recent development. Although it is said that humans have been around for more than 200,000 years, the practice of growing and processing cereal grains such as wheat and rice to make bread, pasta and white rice began only about 2,000 years ago. Before that, humans survived mainly on fruits, meat and fish. An interesting article published in the journal *Human Nutrition* in 2004 has even suggested that the human body has not adapted to the consumption of carbohydrates as a staple food, and I too wonder whether we humans are truly able to digest carbohydrates well.

As a patissier and nutritionist, I considered this research and the foods that my diabetic friend had to avoid, and it inspired me to develop desserts that are low in carbohydrates and made without regular sugar. I started looking into sugar substitutes.

Sugar substitutes appear to be the perfect solution for those who want or need to limit their sugar intake. However, we have to be particular about the kind of substitutes we choose because some of them pose health risks. Generally, there are three major groups of sweeteners. Artificial sweeteners, like saccharin, fall into one group. These are produced synthetically and could potentially have negative effects if taken long term. The second group consists of natural sweeteners extracted from plants. One example is stevia, which is derived from the leaves of a stevia plant. Sugar alcohols make up the last group. Similar to the second group of sweeteners, they are derived from plants or fruits such as apples, strawberries and pears. Sugar is extracted from the plant and combined with hydrogen to form sugar alcohol. Xylitol and sorbitol are examples of sugar alcohol.

The sweetener I chose to use in my recipes is made of a sugar alcohol called erythritol and sugar extracted from monk fruit, also known as *luo han guo*. It is much sweeter than regular sugar, so a little goes a long way.

The friend I mentioned earlier enjoys the desserts that I make often, and continues to have a normal blood sugar level. After meeting countless like-minded people who want to take care of their health and struggle with a long list of foods to avoid, especially desserts, I decided to put together this book. I hope that anyone reading this book will be able to lead a life free of stress when choosing what they want to eat.

Hisae Sakamoto

How to Eat Sweet Treats Without Feeling Guilty

Those with a sweet tooth often wish to indulge in sweet treats without worrying excessively about their weight and health. This book aims to help them and everyone else do just that. Compare the following two strawberry shortcakes.

QUESTION:
Which of these cakes will not make you fat?

A   B

ANSWER:
Cake B

 +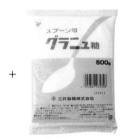

Cake A
Sugar Content: 100.15 g

Cake A was made with refined wheat flour and refined white sugar.

 +

Cake B
Sugar Content: 27.75 g

Cake B was made using soy flour and natural sweetener (page 10, 11).
The recipe is found on page 80.

Both the cakes on the previous page look the same, but they are completely different.

Although counting calories is important, the sugar content in what you eat is even more important. Sugar gives the sweetness in table sugar and fruits, and is also the nutrient that is found in grain ingredients such as flour. Sugar is needed as a source of energy for moving the body, but when taken in excess, the hormone called insulin is overproduced, leading to issues such as diseases and obesity. The collection of dessert recipes in this book does not make use of wheat flour and sugar, and is the answer to a diet low in sugar and free from the stress of having to avoid carbohydrates.

'No Guilt' Desserts

I use this term to refer to desserts that do not contain wheat flour and sugar, and therefore do not make one feel guilty about eating them.

Sugar and the sugar content in wheat flour are the greatest enemies of lifestyle-related diseases, especially diabetes. Through this book, I hope to provide dessert recipes that are healthy, low in sugar, yet delightfully delicious. These desserts use ingredients such as rye flour and maple syrup, which are low-GI[1] and thus will not cause blood sugar levels to increase sharply. Furthermore, without wheat flour, these desserts are low in gluten[2], which is linked to a number of health issues.

These desserts also present low risks in terms of weight gain. While this does not mean that you will lose weight after eating them, you will definitely be able to enjoy these treats without adding to your waistline.

---

[1] This refers to glycemic index value. Foods with low glycemic index value do not cause blood sugar to increase too quickly, thus suppressing the overproduction of insulin and reducing the risk of obesity and diabetes.

[2] This is the protein produced in the endosperm of grains, making them sticky. It is found especially in wheat. Those with gluten intolerance may experience adverse health effects such as digestion problems and headaches if they consume gluten.

Natural sweetener granules   Liquid sweetener   Maple sugar   Maple syrup

Sugar Substitutes

These are the four ingredients I use as substitutes for sugar in this book. They are all plant-based, natural ingredients that are low in calories and sugar content.

Natural Sweetener Granules
This natural sweetener is produced by extracting the sweetness from plants and fruits. There are many varieties of natural sweeteners, but what I use here is a type of sweetener made with a sugar alcohol called erythritol and a fruit called *luo han guo*. The sweetness in this is three times that of sugar (but with zero calories), so using just a small amount will be enough.

Liquid Sweetener
This is natural sweetener granules (see above) in liquid form. Some recipes call for the use of a liquid sweetener.

Maple Sugar and Maple Syrup
Maple syrup is made from boiling sap extracted from the maple tree. When the water content is further removed, maple sugar is formed. Unlike cane sugar and granulated sugar made from sugar cane through refining processes, maple syrup is very natural. It is rich in minerals such as calcium and has a unique richness and fragrance. It is a low-GI ingredient that will not result in a rise in blood sugar level.

Almond meal   Rice flour   Rye flour   Soy flour   Hazelnut meal

Wheat Flour Substitutes

The recipes use mainly nut meals or soy flour. Care has been taken to minimise the amount of ingredients that are high in sugar content.

Almond Meal
This is made of almonds that have been ground very finely. Almond meal is a common ingredient used in dessert-making and its nutty flavour makes desserts even more delicious.

Rice Flour
Although rice flour contains more sugar than wheat flour, it is gluten-free, so we use it sparingly. As rice flour is very fine, there is no need to sift it. It gives a springy texture to desserts.

Rye Flour
Rye belongs to the same plant family as wheat. Although the sugar content and composition is very similar to wheat flour, rye flour has almost no gluten, making it a low-GI food.

Soy Flour
Soy flour is made from grinding soybeans, so it gives a soy flavour to the dish. The sugar content of soy flour is about a fifth of that of wheat flour. Soy is rich in isoflavones and protein that are beneficial for women's health.

Hazelnut Meal
This is made of hazelnuts that have been ground very finely. Rich and nutty in flavour, hazelnut meal is different from almond meal as it has a slightly sweeter flavour.

Other Key Ingredients

These are some of the other ingredients that I use in this book. They can be found in most supermarkets.

EGGS
Eggs appear in most recipes. There are times when the quantity is indicated in grams. As a guide, the weight of one medium egg is about 50 g.

SOY MILK
Unlike cow's milk, which contains high levels of lactose, soy milk is low in sugar and calories. We can also obtain soy isoflavones from soy milk. Look for pure soy milk.

WHIPPING CREAM AND DOUBLE CREAM
I use whipping cream to indicate cream with a fat content of 35%, while double cream indicates cream with a fat content of at least 42%.

COLD-PRESSED SESAME OIL
Cold-pressed sesame oil has no scent or colour. This healthy ingredient has no cholesterol and is used when oil, other than butter, is to be used. Cold-pressed sesame oil produced specifically for dessert-making is also available in supermarkets.

UNSWEETENED CHOCOLATE
You can buy this from baking supply stores. There are some recipes that call for unsweetened chocolate, of which cocoa mass is a raw ingredient.

UNSALTED BUTTER
I use butter without any salt added. Cultured butter is high in sugar, so avoid it. Unsalted butter is an indispensable ingredient as it adds body and a richness to desserts.

CREAM CHEESE
This adds moisture and richness to the texture of cakes. This is, of course, the star ingredient of cheesecakes.

Guidelines

Please keep these points in mind when referring to the recipes in this book:

- The basic unit of measurement for ingredients is in grams (g), and I use millimetres (ml) for certain liquid ingredients. These are limited to the ones for which there are no deviations with the units in grams. As such, you can safely measure in grams the ingredients that are indicated in millimetres.

- Room temperature is assumed to be between 20°C and 25°C.

- In the step-by-step photos, a stand mixer is sometimes shown to be used. However, a hand-held mixer works well too.

- Scrape vanilla seeds from the pods with a knife when a recipe calls for vanilla seeds.

- When a recipe calls for the use of round or rectangular cake tins, ones with removable bases are recommended for easy removal of the dessert. It is for the same reason that many recipes in this book make use of cake rings.

- The temperatures and baking times indicated in this book are based on my domestic electric oven. However, temperature, preheating times and baking times differ for different brands and types of ovens. Use the time indicated as a guide and adjust as needed to your own oven.

- Before using cling film or baking paper products for baking, be sure to read the manufacturer's instructions to confirm the maximum heat-resistant temperature of the product and use it correctly.

- The sugar content stated in each recipe is calculated based on usable carbohydrate content listed in the 2015 Standard Tables of Food Composition in Japan (Ed. 7). The sugar content of the sweetener depends on the brand, so I have not taken that into consideration.

Fail-proof
Basic Desserts
for Beginners

SUGAR CONTENT
Hisae's Recipe
1.55 g
per serving

23.79 g
per serving
Typical Recipe

GÂTEAU AU CHOCOLAT
ガトーショコラ

Makes one 18-cm round cake, serves 8

This gâteau au chocolat is rich but surprisingly light. The egg yolk batter is prepared separately from the meringue. The key to a successful gâteau lies in how you mix the two batters, so if you don't succeed the first time, try again!

INGREDIENTS

Whipping cream (35%) *80 ml*

Unsalted butter *80 g*

Unsweetened chocolate *30 g*

Cold-pressed sesame oil *20 g*

Almond meal *20 g*

Cocoa powder *30 g*

Egg yolks *4*

Natural sweetener granules
25 g + 25 g

Egg whites *4*

NOTE
Sugar is usually added gradually when making a traditional meringue, but when sweeteners are used, the egg whites are first beaten well and the sweetener added all at once following that.

METHOD 350°

1. Preheat oven to 180°C. Prepare an 18-cm round cake tin. Do not grease tin.

2. Heat whipping cream, butter, unsweetened chocolate and sesame oil in a heatproof bowl set over a pot of simmering water until the butter and chocolate are melted. Remove from heat.

3. Sift almond meal and cocoa powder together. Set aside.

4. In a bowl, whisk egg yolks until pale.

5. Add 25 g sweetener and mix well.

6. Add chocolate mixture to egg yolks and whisk until foamy.

7. In another bowl, whisk egg whites until soft peaks form. Add 25 g sweetener and whisk to incorporate.

8. Add one-third of the meringue to the chocolate batter. Mix well with a rubber spatula.

9. Mix in sifted mixture. Add the remaining meringue and mix well with the rubber spatula.

10. Pour batter into prepared cake tin.

11. Bake for about 35 minutes. Remove from the oven and leave the cake to cool before unmoulding.

MUFFINS
マフィン

Makes five 7.5-cm muffins, serves 5

> Cream cheese and apples go exceptionally well together. Desiccated coconut works wonders here too. Indeed, one of the joys of making desserts is finding that perfect match of ingredients.

INGREDIENTS

Apple Flambé

Apple *1*

Cold-pressed sesame oil *5 g*

Natural sweetener granules *20 g*

Unsalted butter *5 g*

Calvados (optional) *10 ml*

Muffins

Cream cheese *80 g, at room temperature*

Unsalted butter *20 g, at room temperature*

Cold-pressed sesame oil *10 ml*

Natural sweetener granules *30 g*

Hazelnut meal *50 g*

Almond meal *30 g*

Desiccated coconut *15 g*

Baking powder *2 g*

Eggs *2, beaten*

Frosting

Double cream (42%) *100 ml*

Natural sweetener granules *5 g*

METHOD

350°

1. Preheat oven to 175°C. Line five 7.5-cm wide muffin moulds with paper muffin cups.

2. Prepare apple flambé. Peel and core apple. Dice into small pieces.

3. Heat sesame oil in a frying pan, then add apple and sweetener. Sauté over medium heat until apple is translucent. Add butter and give the mixture a quick stir.

4. Add Calvados if using and allow the alcohol to evaporate over high heat. Sauté until fragrant and pour mixture onto a tray to cool.

5. Prepare muffins. Combine cream cheese, butter and sesame oil in a bowl and whisk lightly with a hand-held mixer. Add sweetener and continue to whisk lightly until well mixed.

6. Sift in hazelnut meal, almond meal, desiccated coconut and baking powder. Mix well.

7. Add eggs gradually and whisk the batter until pale.

8. Transfer to a piping bag and fill each muffin cup three-quarters full.

9. Divide apple flambé equally among the 5 cups.

10. Bake for about 25 minutes, until muffins are a beautiful golden brown. Remove from the oven and leave to cool.

11. Prepare frosting. In a bowl, whisk frosting ingredients until stiff peaks form. Transfer to a piping bag fitted with a nozzle of your choice and pipe onto cooled muffins.

NOTE
At Step 7, whisk the eggs into the batter more easily by placing the batter over a pot of simmering water.

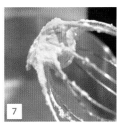

BAKED CHEESECAKE
ベイクドチーズケーキ

Makes one 21 x 8.5-cm cake, serves 7

Simply pour the batter onto the tart crust and bake – that's it! This is a simple method that yields a delicious baked cheesecake.

INGREDIENTS

Tart Crust

Unsalted butter *15 g, chilled + more for greasing*

Almond meal *35 g*

Hazelnut meal *15 g*

Natural sweetener granules *10 g*

Cold-pressed sesame oil *10 g*

Cheese Batter

Cream cheese *220 g*

Natural sweetener granules *20 g*

Whipping cream (35%) *110 ml*

Vanilla seeds *a small amount*

Eggs *2, beaten*

Lemon juice *10 ml*

METHOD 350°

1. Preheat oven to 180°C. Grease a 21 x 8.5-cm cake tin with butter.

2. Prepare tart crust. Combine all tart crust ingredients in a bowl and mix well using a dough scraper.

3. Place crust mixture into prepared cake tin and press down lightly using the dough scraper or a rubber spatula.

4. Bake for 15 minutes. Remove from the oven and leave to cool in the tin. Leave oven heated.

5. Prepare cheese batter. Combine cream cheese, sweetener, whipping cream and vanilla seeds in a heatproof bowl over a pot of simmering water and whisk mixture well until pale.

6. Add eggs in portions, mixing well after each addition. Add lemon juice and continue to mix the batter until thickened.

7. Pour cheese batter onto the tart crust and bake for 40-45 minutes or until a skewer inserted into the centre of the cake comes out clean.

8. Remove from the oven and leave the cake to cool in the tin. Refrigerate for at least 6 hours before serving.

SOUFFLÉ CHEESECAKE
スフレチーズケーキ

Makes one 18-cm round cake, serves 8

Like the gâteau au chocolat, this soft and airy cheesecake uses the same method of preparing the egg yolk and egg white batters separately. The flavour is enhanced with the addition of almond meal towards the end, and the cake holds well even without the use of wheat flour.

INGREDIENTS

Cream cheese *300 g*

Natural sweetener granules *25 g + 25 g*

Whipping cream (35%) *50 ml*

Lemon juice *15 ml*

Cold-pressed sesame oil *10 g*

Egg yolks *3*

Egg whites *3*

Almond meal *15 g*

METHOD   *350*

1. Preheat oven to 180°C. Line an 18-cm round cake tin.

2. Combine cream cheese, 25 g sweetener, whipping cream, lemon juice and sesame oil in a heatproof bowl set over a pot of simmering water. Beat with a hand-held mixer until mixture is smooth.

3. Remove from heat, add egg yolks and beat well.

4. In another bowl, whisk egg whites until soft peaks form. Add 25 g sweetener and mix well.

5. Add meringue to egg yolk mixture and mix lightly with a whisk. Switch to a rubber spatula and stir gently without breaking any bubbles until well mixed. Sift in almond meal and stir until well mixed.

6. Pour batter into prepared cake tin and bake for about 30 minutes.

7. Remove from the oven and leave the cake to cool in the tin. Unmould and chill well before serving.

POUND CAKE
パウンドケーキ

Makes one 18 x 8.5-cm cake, serves 12

This is a pound cake with a difference in taste and texture, thanks to the use of rye flour. Spice in the style of *pain d'épices* (French spice cake) is added to bring out the unique flavour of this pound cake.

INGREDIENTS

Hazelnuts *10 g*

Almonds *10 g*

Pistachios *10 g*

Rye flour *80 g*

Almond meal *80 g*

Maple sugar *50 g*

Baking powder *6 g*

Ground allspice
   (or your favourite spices) *5 g*

Whipping cream (35%) *80 ml*

Eggs *2, beaten*

METHOD

325°

1. Preheat oven to 160°C. Line an 18 x 8.5-cm loaf tin.

2. Place hazelnuts, almonds and pistachios on a baking tray and roast for about 15 minutes. Remove the nuts and set aside to cool. Leave oven heated. Chop cooled nuts roughly.

3. Sift rye flour, almond meal, maple sugar, baking powder and ground allspice together.

4. Add whipping cream and eggs and mix well with a whisk. Mix in chopped nuts.

5. Pour batter into prepared loaf tin and bake for about 50 minutes.

6. Remove from the oven and leave the cake to cool before unmoulding. Slice to serve.

TARTE TATIN
タルトタタン

Makes 10 small tarts, serves 10

The usual tarte tatin, loaded with flour and butter, is never an option for someone on a diet. But how we crave for tarte tatin during the apple season! Try this version of tarte tatin. These petite tarts are not only diet-friendly, they will also invite praises from family and friends with their irresistible appeal.

INGREDIENTS

Caramelised Apple Base

Fuji apples 6 (800 g)

Maple syrup 60 ml

Maple sugar 8 g

Unsalted butter 35 g

Cold-pressed sesame oil 15 g

Pastry

Unsalted butter 50 g, chilled

Rye flour 30 g

Almond meal 30 g

Rice flour 30 g

Salt 1 g

Egg 25 g, beaten

METHOD

1. Preheat oven to 220°C. Prepare 10 silicone muffin cups. Line a baking tray.

2. Prepare caramelised apple base. Peel and core apples. Cut each apple into 12 equal slices.

3. Heat maple syrup and maple sugar in a frying pan over medium heat. Keeping watch the entire time, heat until mixture starts to look caramel-like.

4. Add apple slices, followed by butter and sesame oil. Make a lid with aluminium foil and cook mixture on low heat for about 20 minutes.

5. Using tongs, turn apple slices over and cover with lid again. Continue simmering over low heat for about 10 minutes.

6. Pour caramelised apples equally into prepared muffin cups and bake for about 15 minutes. Lower oven temperature to 200°C and bake for another 20 minutes. Remove from the oven and set aside.

7. Prepare pastry. Place all pastry ingredients except egg in a bowl. Using a dough scraper, mix ingredients well using a chopping motion.

8. Add egg and mix well using the dough scraper.

9. Mix with your fingertips until a dough comes together.

10. Wrap dough in cling film and flatten into a 5-mm thick sheet using a rolling pin. Place in the freezer for about 10 minutes.

11. Remove dough from freezer. Using a 6-cm round cookie cutter, cut out 10 circles.

12. Preheat oven to 180°C.

13. Arrange circles on prepared baking tray and bake for about 20 minutes. Remove from the oven and leave the pastries to cool.

14. Top caramelised apples in each muffin cup with a pastry circle and press down lightly.

15. Place a plate over each mould and turn it over to unmould the tart before serving.

NOTE
Unmould the tarts when they are still slightly warm. They will not be easy to unmould when they have cooled!

SUGAR CONTENT

Hisae's Recipe

4.40 g
per serving

27.30 g
per serving

Typical Recipe

CRUMBLE CAKE
クランブルケーキ

Makes one 16-cm round cake, serves 6

The usual crumble in a crumble cake is made from wheat flour and butter. Here I use diced almonds with rye flour and almond meal to give it an extra crunch. I also add Gorgonzola cheese to the batter to give character to this unique crumble cake.

INGREDIENTS

Crumble

Unsalted butter *25 g, cut into 1-cm cubes and chilled*

Rye flour *5 g*

Almond meal *25 g*

Diced almonds *10 g*

Pistachios *5 g*

Ground cinnamon *2 g*

Maple syrup *5 ml*

Desiccated coconut (optional) *as desired*

Cake Batter

Cream cheese *80 g*

Gorgonzola cheese *10 g*

Cold-pressed sesame oil *10 g*

Unsalted butter *80 g, at room temperature + more for greasing*

Natural sweetener granules *10 g*

Egg *1, beaten*

Almond meal *55 g*

Soy flour *10 g*

Baking powder *2 g*

Raspberry compote *30 g*

METHOD   350°

1. Preheat oven to 180°C. Grease a 16-cm round cake tin with butter.

2. Prepare crumble. In a bowl, mix butter, rye flour, almond meal, almonds, pistachios and cinnamon using a dough scraper.

3. Add maple syrup and mix with your fingertips to form the crumble. Chill crumble in the freezer until you are ready to use it.

4. Prepare cake batter. Heat cream cheese, Gorgonzola cheese and sesame oil in a heatproof bowl set over a pot of simmering water until the mixture is smooth. Remove from heat and leave to cool to room temperature.

5. Add butter and sweetener to the cooled cheese mixture and mix well with a hand-held mixer.

6. Add egg gradually while beating.

7. Sift in almond meal, soy flour and baking powder. Continue to beat until pale.

8. Mix in raspberry compote using a rubber spatula.

9. Pour batter into prepared cake tin and cover with crumble. Bake for about 35 minutes.

10. Remove from the oven. Unmould cake and leave to cool on a wire rack. Garnish with desiccated coconut as desired.

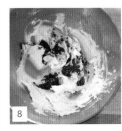

CLAFOUTIS
クラフティ

Makes 6 servings

Soy milk and whipping cream create a perfect balance that is wonderfully smooth on the palate. Prepared delicately, the kirsch cherry adds a touch of tartness to this traditional French dessert.

INGREDIENTS

Cherry Flambé

Unsalted butter *15 g*

Maraschino cherries *12, stems removed*

Kirsch liqueur *10 ml*

Custard

Soy milk *50 ml*

Whipping cream (35%) *150 ml*

Vanilla seeds *a small amount*

Egg *1*

Egg yolk *1*

Cornflour *3 g*

Natural sweetener granules *25 g*

METHOD

1. Preheat oven to 160°C. Prepare six 80-ml ramekins.

2. Prepare cherry flambé. Melt butter in a frying pan, then add cherries and give the mixture a quick stir.

3. Add kirsch liqueur and allow the alcohol to evaporate over high heat. Remove from heat and set aside.

4. Prepare custard. Heat soy milk, whipping cream and vanilla seeds in a saucepan over medium heat until lukewarm (about body temperature).

5. In a bowl, beat egg and egg yolk. Add cornflour and sweetener and beat with a whisk. Continue to whisk while adding soy milk mixture. Strain custard.

6. Pour custard into ramekins until four-fifths full. Place 2 cherries into each ramekin.

7. Bake for about 20 minutes. Remove from the oven and leave the clafoutis to cool before chilling in the refrigerator. Serve chilled.

SUGAR CONTENT

Hisae's Recipe

1.08 g
per serving

12.51 g
per serving

Typical Recipe

GANACHE SANDWICH COOKIES
ガナッシュ

Makes 14 sandwich cookies, serves 14

Ganache is traditionally made with chocolate and whipping cream, but here I use cocoa butter and almond butter to create a praline-style ganache bursting with a nutty flavour. Sandwiching it between cookies similar to macaron shells makes it a combination of all things French.

INGREDIENTS

Almond Batter

Egg white *25 g*

Natural sweetener granules *15 g*

Almond meal *65 g*

Cocoa powder *5 g*

Meringue

Egg white *25 g*

Liquid sweetener *35 g*

Water *20 ml*

Ganache

Cocoa butter *90 g*

Almond butter *100 g*

Whipping cream (35%) *200 ml*

Natural sweetener granules *20 g*

Cold-pressed sesame oil *24 g*

METHOD

1. Preheat oven to 160°C. Line a baking tray.

2. Prepare almond batter. Combine egg white and sweetener in a bowl and sift in almond meal and cocoa powder. Beat with a whisk until well mixed and set aside.

3. Prepare meringue. In a bowl, whisk egg white lightly until bubbles form.

4. Heat sweetener and water in a saucepan until mixture boils.

5. Add boiled mixture gradually to egg white and continue to whisk until the sides of the bowl feel cool.

6. Add meringue to almond batter and mix with a rubber spatula. Transfer to a piping bag fitted with a 9-mm round nozzle. Pipe 28 round shapes, each about 3 cm in diameter, on prepared baking tray.

7. Bake for about 15 minutes. Remove from the oven and leave the cookies to cool on a wire rack.

8. Prepare ganache. Combine all ganache ingredients in a heatproof bowl set over a pot of simmering water. Stir until mixture is melted.

9. Set melted mixture over a bowl of iced water to cool. Using a rubber spatula, continue to stir mixture until emulsified.

10. Transfer to a piping bag fitted with a nozzle of your choice. Pipe on the underside of a cooled cookie and sandwich with another cookie. Repeat with the remaining cookies. Serve.

NOTE
Almond butter is also known as almond paste.

If your hand-held blender has a mill attachment, use this to achieve a smoother mixture at Step 2.

DACQUOISE
ダコワーズ

Makes 7 sandwich cookies, serves 7

A dacquoise is a French dessert cookie with cream sandwiched between layers of almond-flavoured meringue. When I first baked these, I could not help being amazed by how these dessert cookies could be made without sugar! This is definitely one of my favourite desserts.

INGREDIENTS

Dacquoise Cookie

Egg white *100 g*

Natural sweetener granules *15 g + 15 g*

Almond meal *50 g*

Hazelnut meal *20 g*

Cornflour *3 g*

Desiccated coconut *as needed*

Praline Buttercream

Unsalted butter *90 g, at room temperature*

Almond butter *15 g*

Egg white *40 g*

Natural sweetener granules *50 g*

Water *15 g*

METHOD

1. Preheat oven to 160°C. Line a baking tray.

2. Prepare dacquoise cookie. In a bowl, whisk egg white until stiff peaks form. Add 15 g sweetener and mix well.

3. Sift in almond meal, hazelnut meal, cornflour and 15 g sweetener. Mix well with a rubber spatula. Transfer to a piping bag fitted with a 9-mm round nozzle.

4. Pipe on prepared baking tray pairs of 7-cm strips next to each other. Sprinkle with desiccated coconut.

5. Bake for 15-20 minutes or until cookies are golden brown. Remove from the oven and leave the cookies to cool on a wire rack.

6. Prepare praline buttercream. Mix butter and almond butter together and set aside.

7. In another bowl, whisk egg white lightly with a hand-held mixer until bubbles form.

8. Heat sweetener and water in a saucepan over medium heat until mixture simmers. Remove from heat.

9. Add sweetener mixture gradually to beaten egg white and continue to whisk using a hand-held mixer until the sides of the bowl feel cool.

10. Add almond butter mixture and beat until emulsified.

11. Transfer to a piping bag fitted with a nozzle of your choice. Pipe buttercream on the underside of a cooled dacquoise cookie and sandwich with another cookie. Repeat with remaining cookies. Serve.

NOTE
Almond butter is also known as almond paste.

At Step 10, the mixture may separate midway through. Don't worry and just continue to beat!

FINANCIERS
フィナンシェ

Makes 6 mini cakes, serves 6

This is a simple dessert bursting with wonderful buttery flavours. Once you have mastered the technique of creating that brown butter aroma, you will be able to make the most delicious financier you have ever tasted.

INGREDIENTS

Almond meal *50 g*

Cornflour *5 g*

Baking powder *2 g*

Egg white *80 g*

Natural sweetener granules *18 g*

Vanilla seeds *a small amount*

Unsalted butter *45 g + more for greasing*

Cold-pressed sesame oil *15 g*

***Fleur de sel* (hand-harvested sea salt)** *as needed*

METHOD

1. Preheat oven to 160°C. Grease and refrigerate 6 financier moulds.

2. Sift almond meal, cornflour and baking powder together. Add egg white, sweetener and vanilla seeds and whisk well. Set aside.

3. Heat butter and sesame oil in a saucepan over low heat. When butter mixture is light brown, swirl saucepan to carefully brown it slightly further, then remove from heat.

4. Add browned butter to almond meal mixture and mix well.

5. Pour batter into prepared moulds and sprinkle with a small pinch of *fleur de sel*. Bake for about 25 minutes. Remove from the oven and leave the financiers to cool on a wire rack before serving.

CRÈME CARAMEL
プリン

Makes 6 servings

This is a wonderfully rich caramel pudding that is similar to the popular crème brûlée. The caramel is made by slightly caramelising maple syrup, after which a dash of brandy is added for that divine aroma.

INGREDIENTS

Caramel
(amount adjusted for easy preparation)

Maple syrup *80 g*

Water *50 ml*

Brandy *30 ml*

Pudding

Eggs *3*

Milk *200 ml*

Whipping cream (35%) *400 ml*

Natural sweetener granules *35 g*

Vanilla seeds *a small amount*

METHOD *300°*

1. Preheat oven to ~~155~~°C. Prepare hot water and a deep baking tray for water bath baking. Prepare six 120-ml pudding jars.

2. Prepare caramel. Heat maple syrup in a saucepan over medium heat until lightly browned.

3. Remove maple syrup from heat and gradually add water and brandy.

4. Return mixture to heat and mix well until smooth. Remove from heat and set aside.

5. Prepare pudding. Beat eggs in a large bowl.

6. Heat the remaining pudding ingredients in a saucepan over medium heat until mixture is about to boil. Remove from heat and add gradually to eggs, mixing well after each addition.

7. Transfer to a spouted measuring cup and pour into prepared pudding jars until three-quarters full.

8. Place pudding jars on prepared tray and pour hot water into the tray. Bake for 20-25 minutes or until the pudding turns golden. Turn off the oven and leave in the oven for another 10 minutes.

9. Remove from the oven and leave the pudding to cool. Refrigerate to chill before serving with caramel.

CREAM PUFFS
シュークリーム

Makes 6 cream puffs, serves 6

Whenever I ask my students about desserts that seldom turn out well for them, cream puffs always top the list. As such, I came up with this recipe that is fail-proof. I use gelatine to make the custard cream. Be sure to try it out!

INGREDIENTS

Choux Pastry

Unsalted butter *34 g*

Milk *34 ml*

Water *34 ml*

Salt *1 g*

Rice flour *40 g, sifted*

Eggs *2, beaten*

Custard Cream

Milk *100 ml*

Whipping cream (35%) *100 ml*

Vanilla seeds *a small amount*

Egg yolks *2*

Natural sweetener granules *25 g*

Gelatine sheet *6 g, soaked in iced water and drained before using*

Double cream (42%) *180 ml*

Egg Wash

Egg *1, beaten*

METHOD

1. Preheat oven to 250°C. Line a baking tray.

2. Prepare choux pastry. Heat butter, milk, water and salt in a saucepan over medium heat.

3. When mixture comes to a boil, lower the heat and add rice flour.

4. Mix with a rubber spatula. Continue stirring while heating the mixture until a film forms at the bottom of the saucepan.

5. Transfer to a bowl and whisk with a hand-held mixer. Add eggs gradually and mix until well blended and the right consistency is achieved (see Note).

6. Transfer to a piping bag fitted with a 10-mm round nozzle and pipe rounds, each about 5 cm in diameter, on prepared baking tray. Brush rounds with egg wash.

7. Place tray into preheated oven. Turn off the oven and let sit for 5 minutes. Do not open the oven door during this time.

8. Turn on the oven to 180°C and bake for 35 minutes. Remove and leave choux pastries to cool on a wire rack. Once cooled, use a knife to slice a cap off the top of each pastry, about one-quarter from the top.

NOTE
At Step 5, test the consistency by scooping the batter with a spatula, then allowing it to fall back into the bowl. It should form a triangular shape as it falls. Observe carefully as you add the eggs; you may not need to use all the eggs.

At Step 12, test the consistency by dipping a spatula into the custard. If the custard is thick enough to coat the spatula and leave a clear path when you run a finger across it, it is ready.

9. Prepare custard cream. Heat milk, whipping cream and vanilla seeds in a saucepan over medium heat until lukewarm (about body temperature). Remove from heat.

10. In a bowl, combine egg yolks and sweetener and mix well.

11. Add milk mixture gradually and whisk until sweetener is dissolved.

12. Transfer mixture to a saucepan and warm over low heat to 80-85°C, stirring continuously with a rubber spatula until the right consistency is achieved (see Note).

13. Add gelatine and mix well until dissolved. Transfer to a bowl and set over a bowl of iced water to cool.

14. In another bowl, whisk double cream until its lustre is lost.

15. Add gelatine mixture to double cream and mix well with a whisk.

16. Transfer to a piping bag with a nozzle of your choice and pipe into each choux pastry in a circular motion. Replace pastry caps and serve.

Whenever I ask my students about desserts that seldom turn out well for them, cream puffs always top the list. As such, I came up with this recipe that is fail-proof.

ICEBOX COOKIES
アイスボックスクッキー

Makes 45 cookies, serves 45

This is a cookie that I experimented with many times to come up with the perfect balance of rye flour and almond meal. The two different coloured cookie doughs are presented in a stylish chequer pattern.

INGREDIENTS

Maple Cookie Dough

Unsalted butter *50 g, at room temperature*

Maple sugar *20 g*

Rye flour *35 g*

Almond meal *25 g*

Egg yolk *15 g*

Cocoa Cookie Dough

Unsalted butter *50 g, at room temperature*

Maple sugar *20 g*

Rye flour *35 g*

Almond meal *25 g*

Cocoa powder *15 g*

Egg yolk *20 g*

Assembly

Egg white *as needed*

METHOD

1. Preheat oven to 170°C. Line a baking tray.

2. Prepare maple cookie dough. In a bowl, whisk butter and maple sugar until pale.

3. Sift in rye flour and almond meal and continue to mix well. Add egg yolk and continue to mix until dough comes together in a ball.

4. Place dough between 2 sheets of cling film and flatten into a 1-cm thick sheet using a rolling pin. Place in the freezer for about 20 minutes.

5. Prepare cocoa cookie dough as above. Sift in cocoa powder with rye flour and almond meal.

6. Brush one side of the maple cookie dough sheet with some egg white and place cocoa cookie dough sheet over it. With a knife, cut stacked dough into two 1-cm wide strips. Set aside the remaining dough. Brush some egg white on the side of one strip and press the other strip on it to form a chequer pattern.

7. Roll the remaining dough into a ball. Place dough between 2 pieces of cling film and flatten into a 2- to 3-mm thick sheet using a rolling pin. Wrap dough sheet around chequered block, then cover with cling film and place in the freezer for 20 minutes.

8. Cut chilled dough block into 1-cm thick slices and place on prepared baking tray. Bake for 15–20 minutes or until cookies are golden brown. Remove from the oven and leave the cookies to cool on a wire rack before storing or serving.

NOTE
At Step 3, you can also use a food processor to mix the rye flour and almond meal.

SUGAR CONTENT
Hisae's Recipe
8.85 g
per serving

13.35 g
per serving
Typical Recipe

SABLÉS
サブレ

Makes 20 cookies, serves 20

This cookie is as rustic as its name. Mix the dough well and chill it thoroughly before use. The sablé is a classic favourite and you will be reaching for more!

INGREDIENTS

Unsalted butter *100 g, cut into 1-cm cubes and chilled*

Rye flour *150 g*

Rice flour *40 g*

Maple sugar *45 g*

Almond meal *45 g*

Fleur de sel **(hand-harvested sea salt)** *2 g*

Vanilla seeds *a small amount*

Maple syrup *10 g*

Whipping cream (35%) *10 ml*

METHOD

1. Combine butter, rye flour, rice flour, maple sugar, almond meal, *fleur de sel* and vanilla seeds in a bowl. Using a dough scraper, mix ingredients well using a chopping motion.

2. Add maple syrup and whipping cream and mix well using the dough scraper.

3. Gather dough into a ball and roll into a 3-cm thick rod. Wrap in cling film and place in the freezer to rest for 15 minutes.

4. Preheat oven to 170°C. Line a baking tray.

5. With a knife, cut dough into 2-cm thick pieces. Arrange on prepared baking tray. Leave at room temperature for a little while to soften slightly. Use your thumb to create a depression in the middle of softened cookies.

6. Bake for 15–20 minutes or until cookies are golden brown. Remove from the oven and leave cookies to cool on a wire rack before storing or serving.

NOTE
If you have a food processor, you can combine Steps 1 and 2, and place all the ingredients in the processor at once and blend until combined.

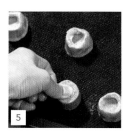

BOULES DE NEIGE (SNOWBALL COOKIES)
ブールドネージュ

Makes 12 cookies, serves 12

The original version uses icing sugar to coat the cookies, making them look like snowballs. Here I have used *kinako* (roasted soybean flour) to create that powdery effect. Crushed walnuts add to that unique flavour that is not found in the usual boules de neige.

INGREDIENTS

Walnuts *25 g*

Unsalted butter *35 g,*
  at room temperature

Almond meal *30 g*

Rice flour *25 g*

Maple sugar *10 g*

Kinako **(roasted soybean flour)** *5 g*

Cold-pressed sesame oil *15 g*

Fleur de sel **(hand-harvested**
  sea salt) *1 g*

Vanilla seeds *a small amount*

METHOD

1. Preheat oven to 160°C. Line a baking tray.

2. Place walnuts on an unlined baking tray and roast for 15 minutes. Set walnuts aside to cool and leave oven heated.

3. Place the remaining ingredients in a bowl and mix well with a hand-held mixer.

4. Place cooled walnuts between 2 sheets of baking paper and crush into coarse bits using a rolling pin. Add to dough and mix well.

5. Roll dough into balls, each about 13 g and 2 cm in diameter. Place on lined baking tray.

6. Bake for 20-25 minutes or until cookies are golden brown. Remove from the oven and leave the cookies to cool on a wire rack before storing or serving.

CRÊPES
クレープ

Makes nine 15-cm crêpes, serves 9

Even for those who don't really like the unique fragrance of soybeans in soy milk, the sweet aroma of buckwheat in this crêpe is really hard to resist. Delicious brown butter adds another dimension to the crêpes.

INGREDIENTS

Crêpes

Unsalted butter *75 g*

Buckwheat flour *100 g*

Egg *25 g, beaten*

Natural sweetener granules *10 g*

Soy milk *400 ml*

Water *130 ml*

Rum *10 ml*

Salt *1 g*

Cold-pressed sesame oil
as needed

Filling

Double cream (42%) *200 ml*

Natural sweetener granules *10 g*

Strawberries *9*

Decoration

Your choice of fruit compote
as desired

Mint leaves *as desired*

METHOD

1. Prepare crêpes. Heat butter in a saucepan over low heat, swirling until it is a burnt brown colour. Pour into a bowl and leave to cool.

2. In another bowl, combine buckwheat flour, egg, sweetener, soy milk, water, rum and salt. Whisk lightly to combine.

3. Add in browned butter and mix further.

4. Pour into another bowl and refrigerate for about 1 hour.

5. Heat a frying pan over low heat and brush with a thin layer of sesame oil using a paper towel.

6. Pour in a small amount of batter and spread it as thinly and evenly as possible. When the underside of the crêpe is golden brown, flip it over to cook the other side. Remove to a plate to cool. Repeat to make 9 crêpes.

7. Prepare filling. In a bowl, whisk double cream and sweetener until stiff peaks form.

8. Spread some filling on a cooled crêpe, place a strawberry in the centre and roll up the crêpe. Repeat with the remaining crêpes and filling. Arrange crêpes on a plate and garnish with fruit compote and sprigs of mint as desired.

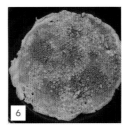

SCONES
スコーン

Makes seven 6-cm scones, serves 7

I created these low-sugar scones based on a recipe from a friend who was brought up in England. Do enjoy it with deliciously rich clotted cream (with about 60% milk fat content).

INGREDIENTS

Unsalted butter *30 g, chilled*

Rye flour *100 g*

Rice flour *30 g*

Almond meal *70 g*

Baking powder *8 g*

Salt *1 g*

Egg *1*

Whipping cream (35%) *50 ml*

Cold-pressed sesame oil *15 g*

Water *35 ml*

Clotted cream *30 g*

Your choice of fruit compote *30 g*

Egg Wash

Egg *1, beaten*

METHOD

1. Preheat oven to 220°C. Line a baking tray.

2. Place butter in a bowl and cut it up with a dough scraper.

3. Sift in rye flour, rice flour, almond meal, baking powder and salt. Mix ingredients well using a chopping motion.

4. Add egg, whipping cream, sesame oil and water. Using the dough scraper, mix until a dough comes together.

5. Form dough into a ball and wrap in cling film. Flatten using your hands into a 2.5-cm thick disc.

6. Rest dough in the refrigerator for about 30 minutes.

7. Using a 6-cm round cookie cutter, cut out circles from dough. Brush with egg wash and place on prepared tray.

8. Bake for 20–25 minutes or until scones are golden brown. Remove from the oven. Leave the scones to cool before serving with clotted cream and your choice of fruit compote.

BROWNIES
ブラウニー

Makes one 16 x 10-cm cake, serves 8

The brownie is such an easy dessert to make – simply mix and bake.
Cut it up into cubes, decorate it and you will have the perfect gift.

INGREDIENTS

Cream cheese *50 g*

Unsalted butter *30 g*

Cold-pressed sesame oil *10 g*

Unsweetened chocolate *30 g*

Almond meal *100 q*

Cocoa powder *30 g*

Natural sweetener granules *45 g*

Salt *1 g*

Eggs *2*

Decoration

Walnuts *8*

Unsweetened chocolate *10 g*

METHOD   35⁰

1. Preheat oven to 175°C. Line a 16 x 10-cm cake tin.

2. Heat cream cheese, butter, sesame oil and chocolate in a heatproof
    bowl set over a pot of simmering water until mixture is smooth.
    Remove from heat.

3. In another bowl, sift almond meal, cocoa powder, sweetener and
    salt together.

4. Beat eggs and add gradually to sifted mixture. Mix well with a whisk.

5. Add cream cheese mixture and continue to mix. Pour batter into
    prepared cake tin. Arrange walnuts evenly in 2 rows on the batter
    so that when the brownie is divided into 8 pieces, each serving has
    a walnut.

6. Bake for about 30 minutes. Remove from the oven and leave the
    brownie to cool.

7. Remove brownie from the tin before cutting in half horizontally.
    Divide each half further into 4 equal pieces (about 4 × 5 cm each).

8. Melt chocolate in a heatproof bowl set over a pot of simmering
    water, then transfer to a piping cornet made from baking paper.
    Pipe chocolate over brownies.

NOTE
*A piping cornet is a conical piping bag
used to create fine lines on desserts.*

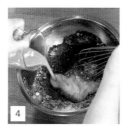

MADELEINES
マドレーヌ

Makes five 6-cm madeleines, serves 5

This is a favourite with most Japanese and will also appeal to those who like rum. I hope you will enjoy it too.

INGREDIENTS

Unsalted butter *50 g, at room temperature*

Cream cheese *30 g, at room temperature*

Natural sweetener granules *15 g*

Vanilla seeds *a small amount*

Egg *1, beaten*

Almond meal *70 g*

Rum *3 ml*

Sliced almonds *as desired*

METHOD

1. Preheat oven to 170°C. Prepare five 6-cm wide madeleine cups.

2. Place butter, cream cheese, sweetener and vanilla seeds into a bowl and mix well with a rubber spatula.

3. Add egg gradually to butter mixture and mix well with a whisk to incorporate air bubbles.

4. Sift in almond meal and add rum. Mix well to incorporate air bubbles.

5. Transfer to a piping bag without a nozzle and pipe into prepared madeleine cups. Top each cup with some sliced almonds.

6. Bake for about 25 minutes. Remove from the oven and leave the madeleines to cool on a wire rack before serving.

SUGAR CONTENT

Hisae's Recipe

1.13 g
per serving

14.45 g
per serving

Typical Recipe

BAUMKUCHEN
バウムクーヘン

Makes one 20-cm roll, serves 8

Baumkuchen is a dessert I enjoy eating and I have always thought of making for myself. This is my version – a simple yet delightful cake that can be made by simply baking in a large tray and rolling it up.

INGREDIENTS

Maple syrup *10 g*

Rum *10 ml*

Cream cheese *15 g*

Cold-pressed sesame oil *10 g*

Eggs *3*

Natural sweetener granules *25 g*

Soy flour *10 g*

Agar powder *2 g*

METHOD

1. Preheat oven to 180°C. Line a 40 x 30-cm baking tray.

2. In a bowl, combine maple syrup and rum. Mix well and set aside.

3. Heat cream cheese and sesame oil in a heatproof bowl set over a pot of simmering water until cream cheese is melted. Remove from heat.

4. In a bowl, whisk eggs with a hand-held mixer until pale. When eggs are frothy, add sweetener and continue to whisk.

5. Add cream cheese mixture and whisk lightly.

6. Add soy flour and agar powder and mix well with a rubber spatula.

7. Pour batter into prepared baking tray and spread it out thinly using a palette knife. Bake for about 10 minutes.

8. Remove from the oven. Take the cake out of the tray immediately and brush evenly with maple syrup mixture.

9. Cut cake into half along its breadth. From its shorter edge, roll up the first half tightly. Place the roll on the shorter edge of the second half and roll up tightly again. Cut into 8 slices.

Scan this QR code to watch a video tutorial on rolling up Baumkuchen.

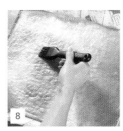

Tarts and Sponge Cakes

BASIC TART CRUST
基本のタルト台

Makes two 12-cm crusts or one 18-cm crust

If you know how to make this tart crust, you will be able to make tarts with various fillings such as seasonal fruits, chocolate and cheese. The almond and hazelnut flavours are balanced very well in this tart crust.

INGREDIENTS

Unsalted butter *50 g, at room temperature*

Almond meal *110 g*

Hazelnut meal *35 g*

Natural sweetener granules *25 g*

Cold-pressed sesame oil *10 g*

METHOD

1. Preheat oven to 180°C. Prepare two 12-cm tart tins or an 18-cm round cake ring.

2. Place all ingredients except sesame oil in a bowl. Using a dough scraper, mix ingredients well using a chopping motion.

3. When mixture is well combined, add sesame oil. Mix and knead until the dough can be gathered into a ball.

4. If using the 12-cm tart tins, divide dough into 2 portions and press evenly into the base and up the sides of each tart tin. If using an 18-cm cake ring, place it on a lined baking tray and press the dough onto the baking tray, using the cake ring to keep the crust round.

5. Place a sheet of baking paper over the dough and place pie weights on it. Bake for 15–20 minutes. Remove from the oven and leave to cool. The tart crust may break apart easily when it is warm, so avoid touching it and unmould it only after it is cool.

STRAWBERRY PISTACHIO TART
いちごとピスタチオのタルト

Makes one 12-cm tart, serves 4

The pale green pistachio filling goes really well with strawberries. Top it off with a sprinkle of pistachio bits against the bright red strawberries, and get ready for a feast for the eyes and the palate.

INGREDIENTS

12-cm Basic Tart Crust (page 62) 1

Pistachio Filling

Unsalted butter 40 g, at room temperature

Pistachio meal 45 g

Natural sweetener granules 16 g

Rum 5 ml

Egg 35 g, beaten

Decoration

Double cream (42%) 100 ml

Natural sweetener granules 5 g

Strawberries 10, washed and hulled

Pistachios about 5, roughly chopped

METHOD

350°

1. Preheat oven to 180°C.

2. Prepare pistachio filling. Place all ingredients except egg in a bowl and whisk. Add egg gradually and whisk until mixture is pale.

3. Pour filling onto tart crust and level it out.

4. Bake for 20–25 minutes. Remove from the oven and leave the tart to cool in the tin.

5. Prepare decoration. Place double cream and sweetener in a bowl and whisk until stiff peaks form. Transfer to a piping bag fitted with a nozzle of your choice and pipe cream around the tart.

6. Place 4 whole strawberries on the centre of the tart. Quarter the remaining strawberries and arrange decoratively on the tart. Sprinkle with pistachios and serve.

NOTE
When piping the cream, I like using a large St Honore piping tip. I also find that piping the cream towards the centre of the tart makes a pretty design.

Scan this QR code to watch a video tutorial on piping cream onto Strawberry Pistachio Tart.

BLUEBERRY CREAM CHEESE TART
ブルーベリーレアチーズタルト

Makes one 18-cm tart, serves 8

This is a really simple recipe. If you bake the tart crust beforehand, the only thing left to do is pour in the cream cheese mousse. Despite its simplicity, the final product is nothing short of gorgeous.

INGREDIENTS

18-cm Basic Tart Crust (page 62) *1*

Cream Cheese Mousse

Cream cheese *200 g*

Plain yoghurt (sugar-free) *50 g*

Natural sweetener granules *30 g*

Whipping cream (35%) *30 ml + 200 ml*

Lemon juice *15 ml*

Gelatine sheet *7 g, soaked in iced water and drained before using*

Blueberry Jelly

Natural sweetener granules *5 g*

Lemon juice *10 ml*

Water *100 ml*

Blueberries *about 50*

Gelatine sheet *5 g, soaked in iced water and drained before using*

METHOD

1. Place prepared tart crust into the base of an 18-cm round springform tin or prepare it in the springform tin.

2. Prepare cream cheese mousse. Combine cream cheese, yoghurt, sweetener, 30 ml whipping cream, lemon juice and gelatine in a heatproof bowl. Set over a pot of simmering water until mixture is melted. Let mixture cool to room temperature.

3. In another bowl, whisk 200 ml whipping cream until soft peaks form.

4. Add cream cheese mixture to whipping cream and, alternating between using a whisk and a spatula, mix until well combined. Pour cream cheese mousse onto the tart crust and lightly knock the tin on a hard surface to remove any air bubbles. Place in the freezer to set.

5. Prepare blueberry jelly. Heat sweetener, lemon juice and water in a saucepan over medium heat until mixture is about to boil.

6. Add blueberries and continue to cook until the colour from the blueberries has seeped out. Remove from heat. Add gelatine and mix well until dissolved. Set over a bowl of iced water and let mixture cool to room temperature.

7. Pour cooled mixture onto set tart. Arrange blueberries neatly on top of tart and refrigerate for about 30 minutes.

8. Unmould chilled tart and slice to serve.

NOTE
Unmoulding the tart will be easier if you warm the sides of the tin up slightly using a warm wet towel.

LEMON TARTS
レモンタルト

Makes five 6-cm tarts

The tartness of lemons makes this a perfect after-meal dessert. It's simple to make, yet so delightfully delicious.

INGREDIENTS

Basic Tart Crust dough (page 62)
¹/₂ portion

Lemon Mousse

Agar powder *1 g*

Natural sweetener granules *25 g*

Lemon juice *50 ml*

Lemon zest *of ¹/₃ lemon, grated*

Egg *1*

Egg yolk *1*

Unsalted butter *50 g, chilled*

Jelly

Natural sweetener granules *5 g*

Water *50 ml*

Gelatine sheet *2 g, soaked in iced water and drained before using*

Lemon slices *5*

METHOD

1. Divide the tart crust dough into 6 portions and press each portion into a 6-cm round cake ring on a lined baking tray.

2. Prepare lemon mousse. Combine agar powder and sweetener in a heatproof bowl and mix well.

3. Mix in lemon juice and lemon zest. Add egg and egg yolk and beat lightly. Set over a pot of simmering water and continue beating mixture until thickened. Remove from heat and leave to cool to about body temperature.

4. Add butter and mix well with a whisk. Pour lemon mousse evenly onto prepared tart crusts and refrigerate 20-30 minutes to set.

5. Prepare jelly. Heat sweetener and water in a saucepan over medium heat. When mixture is about to come to a boil, turn off the heat. Add gelatine and mix until dissolved.

6. Leave mixture to cool until slightly lower than body temperature. Pour onto chilled tarts and refrigerate for 20-30 minutes to set. Unmould tarts and garnish with lemon slices before serving.

SUGAR CONTENT
Hisae's Recipe
4.89 g
per serving

21.33 g
per serving
Typical Recipe

FLORENTINES
フロランタン

Makes one 21 x 8.5-cm pastry, serves 7

One can never get enough of the delicious flavour of almonds. The maple syrup flavour in this florentine makes it a dessert that is truly unforgettable.

INGREDIENTS

Basic Tart Crust dough (page 62)
¹/₂ portion

Filling

Maple sugar *15 g*

Maple syrup *20 g*

Whipping cream (35%) *60 ml*

Unsalted butter *20 g*

Sliced almonds *60 g*

METHOD

1. Preheat oven to 180°C. Line a 21 x 8.5-cm baking tray.

2. Prepare tart crust. Flatten dough into a 3-mm thick sheet and place in prepared baking tray. Bake for 15–20 minutes. Remove from the oven and leave to cool in tray. Lower oven temperature to 170°C.

3. Prepare filling. Place all filling ingredients except sliced almonds in a saucepan over medium heat. Keep stirring until ingredients are dissolved and mixture is thickened.

4. Add sliced almonds and cook until the mixture is sticky.

5. Pour filling onto prepared tart crust and bake for 20–25 minutes. Remove from the oven and leave to cool in tray. Slice to serve.

PEACH TART
桃のタルト

Makes one 12-cm tart, serves 4

> Peach is a fruit that is relatively low in sugar and is therefore lower in calories. It is said to reduce fluid retention and increase metabolism. Do try this recipe during the peach season!

INGREDIENTS

12-cm Basic Tart Crust (page 62) *1, unbaked*

Stewed peaches *2*

Crème d'Amande
(Sweet Almond Paste)

Unsalted butter *30 g, at room temperature*

Almond meal *30 g*

Natural sweetener granules *10 g*

Vanilla seeds *a small amount*

Egg *55 g, beaten*

Custard Cream

Milk *50 ml*

Whipping cream (35%) *50 ml*

Vanilla seeds *a small amount*

Egg yolk *1*

Natural sweetener granules *15 g*

Gelatine sheet *3.5 g, soaked in iced water and drained before using*

Decoration

Chervil *1 sprig*

METHOD

1. Preheat oven to 180°C.

2. Prepare crème d'amande. Place all crème d'amande ingredients except egg in a bowl and mix with a whisk.

3. Add egg to mixture and whisk until pale.

4. Pour crème d'amande onto prepared tart crust. Cut a stewed peach in half, then cut each half into bite-sized pieces. Press pieces gently into the tart.

5. Bake for about 35 minutes. Leave the tart to cool before unmoulding.

6. Prepare custard cream. Heat milk, whipping cream and vanilla seeds in a saucepan over medium heat until lukewarm (about body temperature). Remove from heat.

7. In another bowl, combine egg yolk and sweetener and mix well.

8. Add milk mixture gradually to egg yolk mixture and whisk until sweetener is dissolved.

9. Transfer mixture to a saucepan and warm over low heat to 80–85°C, stirring continuously with a rubber spatula until the mixture is thick enough to coat the back of the spatula and leave a clear path when you run a finger across it.

10. Add gelatine and mix well until dissolved. Transfer custard cream to a bowl and set over a bowl of iced water to cool.

11. Transfer to a piping bag with a nozzle of your choice and pipe custard cream onto the tart crust.

12. Cut the remaining peach into bite-sized pieces and decorate the tart as desired. Top with a sprig of chervil before serving.

BASIC SPONGE CAKE
基本のスポンジ生地

Makes one 33 x 23-cm cake

This sponge cake uses whipped egg whites and is thus a type of soufflé sponge. You can make a fluffy roll with this. Normally, this batter is not suitable for shortcakes, but when it is baked as a sheet cake and skilfully assembled, it will be able to withstand weight.

INGREDIENTS

Cream cheese *70 g*

Cold-pressed sesame oil *10 g*

Egg yolks *5*

Natural sweetener granules
   25 g + 25 g

Egg whites *4*

Soy flour *15 g*

METHOD 350°

1. Preheat oven to 180°C. Line a 33 x 23-cm baking tray.

2. Heat cream cheese and sesame oil in a heatproof bowl set over a pot of simmering water until mixture is smooth. Remove from heat.

3. In another heatproof bowl set over a pot of simmering water, whisk egg yolks with a hand-held mixer until mixture is light and egg yolks are pale.

4. Add 25 g sweetener and continue to mix. Add cream cheese mixture and mix lightly.

5. In another bowl, whisk egg whites with a hand-held mixer until stiff peaks form. Add 25 g sweetener and continue to mix well.

6. Add half the meringue to the cream cheese mixture and mix well with a whisk.

7. Sift in soy flour and fold in with a spatula. Add the remaining meringue and mix well, taking care not to break the air bubbles.

8. Pour batter into prepared baking tray and smoothen with a palette knife. Bake for 10–13 minutes until golden brown. Remove from the oven and leave to cool on a wire rack.

NOTE
Sugar is usually added gradually when making a traditional meringue, but when sweeteners are used, the egg whites are first beaten well and the sweetener added all at once following that.

BUTTER ROLL CAKE
バターロールケーキ

Makes one 33-cm roll cake, serves 8

Filled with a rich cream that is made with plenty of butter, this cake is a hot favourite among my customers. Use the best grade of butter you can find as the scrumptiousness of the butter roll cake depends very much on the type of butter used.

INGREDIENTS

Basic Sponge Cake (page 74)
1, still lined with baking paper

Buttercream

Unsalted butter *240 g, at room temperature*

Vanilla seeds *a small amount*

Natural sweetener granules *30 g*

Water *20 ml*

Egg *1*

Caramelised Almonds
(use 10 g and store the rest)

Diced almonds *100 g*

Maple syrup *10 g*

Unsalted butter *5 g*

Decoration

Boiled sweet black beans (store-bought) *15, drained*

> NOTE
> *At Step 5, the mixture may separate, but continue whisking until it emulsifies.*

Scan this QR code to watch a video tutorial on rolling up Butter Roll Cake.

METHOD

1. Prepare buttercream. Mix butter and vanilla seeds together and set aside.

2. Heat sweetener and water in a saucepan for 1 minute.

3. Place egg in a bowl and whisk with a hand-held mixer until bubbles form. Add heated mixture gradually and continue to stir until cooled.

4. Add butter mixture to egg mixture gradually and continue mixing until combined.

5. Prepare caramelised almonds. Roast diced almonds in a 160°C-oven for about 15 minutes.

6. Heat maple syrup in a saucepan over medium heat. When mixture starts to boil, add roasted almonds. Move the saucepan continuously over the heat until mixture is caramelised.

7. Turn off the heat and add butter. Mix well and spread almonds on a sheet of baking paper to cool.

8. Assemble cake. Using a long serrated knife, trim the longer edges of the cake at a slant. Make shallow cuts 1-cm apart down the length of the cake, leaving a 5-cm margin on one side. Turn the cake so a long edge faces you.

9. Spoon two-thirds of the buttercream onto the cake and spread evenly with a palette knife.

10. Arrange black beans in a line about 5 cm from one long edge of the cake.

11. Holding on to the edge of the baking paper, roll the cake up, away from you, tightly. Refrigerate for about 5 minutes to chill.

12. Spread the remaining buttercream neatly on the roll cake. Refrigerate for another 5 minutes to chill.

13. Decorate with 10 g caramelised almonds and slice to serve.

MATCHA ROLL CAKE
抹茶ロールケーキ

Makes one 33-cm roll cake, serves 8

The key to making a good matcha dessert is temperature. In order to bring out the flavour of matcha, this recipe requires neither high temperatures nor heating for a long period of time. The matcha powder used to decorate this cake also works wonders.

INGREDIENTS

Matcha Sponge Cake

Soy flour *10 g*

Uji matcha powder *8 g*

Cream cheese *70 g*

Cold-pressed sesame oil *10 g*

Egg yolks *5*

Natural sweetener granules
   25 g + 25 g

Egg whites *4*

Cream

Double cream (42%) *200 ml*

Natural sweetener granules *10 g*

Decoration

Uji matcha powder *as desired*

NOTE
Uji is a region in Japan that is well known for its green tea. If unavailable, replace with any other unsweetened matcha powder.

Scan this QR code to watch a video tutorial on decorating Matcha Roll Cake.

METHOD

1. Preheat oven to 180°C. Line a 33 x 23-cm baking tray.

2. Prepare matcha sponge cake. Sift soy flour and matcha powder together and mix with a whisk. Set aside.

3. Heat cream cheese and sesame oil in a heatproof bowl set over a pot of simmering water until mixture is smooth. Remove from heat.

4. In another heatproof bowl set over a pot of simmering water, whisk egg yolks with a hand-held mixer until mixture is light and egg yolks are pale.

5. Add 25 g sweetener and continue to mix. Add cream cheese mixture and mix lightly.

6. In another bowl, whisk egg whites with a hand-held mixer until stiff peaks form. Add 25 g sweetener and continue to mix well.

7. Add half the meringue to the cream cheese mixture. Switch to a whisk and mix well.

8. Fold in matcha powder mixture using a rubber spatula. Add the remaining meringue and mix well, taking care not to break the air bubbles.

9. Pour batter into prepared baking tray and smoothen with a palette knife. Bake for 10–13 minutes. Remove from the oven and leave to cool with the baking paper attached.

10. Prepare cream. Place double cream and sweetener in a bowl and whisk until stiff peaks form.

11. Assemble cake. Using a long serrated knife, trim the longer edges of the cake at a slant. Make shallow cuts 1-cm apart down the length of the cake, leaving a 5-cm margin on one side. Turn the cake so a long edge faces you.

12. Spoon cream onto the cake and spread evenly with a palette knife.

13. Holding on to the edge of the baking paper, roll the cake up, away from you, tightly. Refrigerate for about 5 minutes to chill.

14. Use a ruler or a sheet of paper to cover the sides, then sprinkle matcha powder to make a 2-cm wide strip on the top of the roll. Slice to serve.

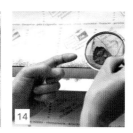

STRAWBERRY SHORTCAKE
いちごのショートケーキ

Makes one 12-cm round cake, serves 4

With a smaller diameter, this three-tiered, six-layered soufflé shortcake is able to withstand the weight of the cream and strawberries. Try different types of piping nozzles to come up with attractive designs.

INGREDIENTS

Basic Sponge Cake (page 74) *1*

Syrup

Liquid sweetener *10 g*

Water *10 ml*

Decoration

Strawberries *14, washed and hulled*

Double cream (42%) *150 ml*

Natural sweetener granules *7.5 g + 7.5 g*

Whipping cream (35%) *200 ml*

Chervil *a few sprigs*

METHOD

1. Using a 12-cm cake ring, cut out 3 round pieces from sponge cake.

2. Prepare syrup. Mix sweetener and water together. Set aside.

3. Prepare strawberries for decoration. Cut 7 strawberries into halves. Set aside.

4. Prepare cream for decoration. Place double cream and 7.5 g sweetener in a bowl and whisk until stiff peaks form.

5. Brush syrup on one side of one cake layer. This will be the base layer. Brush syrup on both sides for the remaining 2 cake layers.

6. Place the base cake layer on a cake board. Spoon some whisked double cream on it and spread with a palette knife. Arrange 7 strawberry halves on top and cover with more double cream.

7. Place a second cake layer over and repeat the process of layering. Place the last cake layer on top.

8. Smoothen the cream around the sides of the cake and spread a thin layer of the remaining double cream on the top. Refrigerate to set cream. Chilling the cream will also ensure that when the cake is coated with whipping cream (Step 10), it will appear smoother.

9. Place whipping cream and 7.5 g sweetener in a bowl and whisk until soft peaks form.

10. Spoon two-thirds of the whipping cream on the cake and spread evenly around the sides and top of the cake using a palette knife.

11. Whisk the remaining whipping cream until stiff peaks form. Transfer to a piping bag fitted with a nozzle of your choice and pipe cream around the circumference of the cake. Arrange the remaining strawberries in the centre. Garnish with sprigs of chervil.

NOTE
When smoothening the cream around the cake at Step 8, it is fine if the cake layers are still visible. You just need to spread the cream thinly at this point.

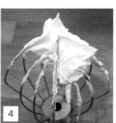

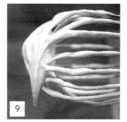

SUGAR CONTENT

Hisae's Recipe

3.85 g
per serving

40.57 g
per serving

Typical Recipe

BLACK FOREST CAKE
フォレノワール

Makes one 15-cm round cake, serves 8

The black forest cake, known as *gâteau de forêt noire* in French, originated in Germany. The perfect combination of cherries, cocoa and whipping cream makes this an all-time favourite amongst adults.

INGREDIENTS

Cocoa Sponge Cake

Cream cheese *65 g*

Cold-pressed sesame oil *15 g*

Soy flour *10 g*

Cocoa powder *8 g*

Egg yolks *5*

Natural sweetener granules
25 g + 25 g

Egg whites *4*

Chocolate Mousse

Unsweetened chocolate *50 g*

Cold-pressed sesame oil *20 g*

Egg yolks *2*

Whipping cream (35%)
50 ml + 125 ml

Natural sweetener granules *20 g*

Gelatine sheet *5 g, soaked in iced water and drained before using*

Decoration

Maraschino cherries *about 15*

Double cream (42%) *150 ml*

Natural sweetener granules *10 g*

Kirsch liqueur (optional) *10 ml*

Cocoa powder *as desired*

Cocoa nibs *as desired*

METHOD

1. Preheat oven to 180°C. Line a 33 x 23-cm baking tray.

2. Prepare cocoa sponge cake. Heat cream cheese and sesame oil in a heatproof bowl set over a pot of simmering water until mixture is smooth. Remove from heat.

3. Sift soy flour and cocoa powder together and mix with a whisk. Set aside.

4. In a heatproof bowl set over a pot of simmering water, whisk egg yolks with a hand-held mixer until mixture is light and egg yolks are pale.

5. Add 25 g sweetener and continue to mix. Add cream cheese mixture and mix lightly.

6. In another bowl, whisk egg whites with a hand-held mixer until stiff peaks form. Add 25 g sweetener and continue to mix well.

7. Add half the meringue to the cream cheese mixture, switch to a whisk, and mix well.

8. Add soy flour mixture and fold in with a rubber spatula. Add the remaining meringue and mix well, taking care not to break the air bubbles.

9. Pour batter into prepared baking tray and smoothen with a palette knife. Bake for 10–13 minutes. Remove from the oven and leave to cool on a wire rack.

10. Prepare chocolate mousse. Follow Steps 7–13 on page 92, but do not transfer to a piping bag.

11. Using a 15-cm cake ring, cut out 2 round pieces of cocoa sponge cake. You may also combine 2 halves (see photo).

12. Prepare a cake board and place the 15-cm cake ring on top of it.

13. Place a cake layer inside the cake ring and pour half the chocolate mousse over it. Arrange 8 cherries on top and pour in the remaining chocolate mousse.

14. Place the second cake layer on top and refrigerate for 20–30 minutes to set mousse.

15. Prepare decoration. Place double cream, sweetener and kirsch liqueur in a bowl and whisk until stiff peaks form.

16. Remove cake ring and spread two-thirds of double cream over cake.

17. Transfer remaining double cream to a piping bag fitted with a nozzle of your choice. Arrange remaining cherries in the centre of the cake and pipe cream around cherries.

18. Dust cake with cocoa powder and sprinkle cocoa nibs around the sides as desired.

COCOA BUTTER WHITE RAW CHOCOLATES
カカオバターで作るホワイト生チョコレート

Yield varies depending on size

Store-bought white chocolates tend to be very sweet because they are usually made with more sugar than cocoa butter. As a result, the subtle cocoa flavour is lost. Try making this version.

INGREDIENTS

Cocoa butter *50 g*

Evaporated milk *23 g*

Natural sweetener granules *10 g*

Whipping cream (35%) *50 ml*

Cold-pressed sesame oil *12 g*

Desiccated coconut *a little*

METHOD

1. Prepare a baking tray.

2. Combine all ingredients except desiccated coconut in a heatproof bowl and set over a pot of simmering water until mixture is smooth.

3. Beat mixture with a hand-held mixer until emulsified.

4. Remove from heat and set over a bowl of iced water. Using a rubber spatula, mix gently, taking care that air does not get incorporated into the mixture.

5. When mixture is at a consistency that is easy to pipe, transfer to a piping bag with a nozzle of your choice. Pipe shapes onto prepared baking tray. Refrigerate to set chocolate.

6. Decorate with desiccated coconut.

Chilled Desserts

TIRAMISU
ティラミス

Makes 6 servings

The key here is to handle the eggs gently so as to get a rich cream.
It may take a little more work, but please try out this authentic tiramisu
without sugar.

INGREDIENTS

Basic Sponge Cake (page 74) *1*

Mascarpone Cream

Egg *1*

Egg yolk *1*

Natural sweetener granules *20 g*

Water *10 ml*

Gelatine sheet *1.5 g, soaked in
   iced water and drained before
   using*

Mascarpone cheese *110 g*

Whipping cream (35%) *150 ml*

Syrup

Coffee beans *15 g, ground*

Water *40 ml + 20 ml*

Liquid sweetener *15 g*

Rum *20 ml*

Decoration

Cocoa powder *60 g*

Coffee beans *6*

METHOD

1. Prepare six 4.5-cm wide serving glasses.

2. Using a serving glass as a size reference, cut 18 round pieces from
   the sponge cake. The remaining sponge cake can be frozen for use in
   other recipes.

3. Prepare mascarpone cream. Mix egg and egg yolk in a bowl with a
   hand-held mixer until fluffy.

4. Heat sweetener and water in a saucepan over medium heat.
   When it comes to a boil, pour in egg mixture. Beat mixture with a
   hand-held mixer until cooled.

5. Combine gelatine and mascarpone cheese in a heatproof bowl set
   over a pot of simmering water and whisk until smooth. Add egg
   mixture and continue to whisk mixture while heated until combined.
   Leave to chill until slightly cooler than room temperature.

6. Whisk whipping cream until soft peaks form. Fold into cream cheese
   mixture using a rubber spatula. Transfer to a piping bag (without a
   nozzle) and set aside.

7. Prepare syrup. Heat ground coffee beans and 40 ml water in a
   saucepan over medium heat. When mixture comes to a boil, turn off
   the heat and filter through a coffee filter. Mix in sweetener and rum,
   followed by 20 ml water.

8. Assemble tiramisu. Dip a sponge cake round into the syrup,
   squeeze lightly and place in a prepared serving glass. Pipe in some
   mascarpone cream and sift some cocoa powder onto it using a tea
   strainer. Repeat to add another 2 layers of cake, cream and cocoa
   powder, then top with a coffee bean. Repeat with the remaining
   ingredients to make another 5 glasses. Refrigerate to chill
   before serving.

CRÈME D'ANJOU
クレーム・ダンジュ

Makes 5 servings

Just leave overnight and you will have delightful crème d'anjou that is just as good as any store-bought version. The fluffy texture and the refreshing taste of fromage blanc make this a truly enjoyable dessert.

INGREDIENTS

Fromage blanc *150 g*

Lemon zest *of ¹/₂ lemon, grated*

Natural sweetener granules
5 g + 5 g

Cointreau *10 ml*

Double cream (45%) *125 ml*

Egg white *60 g*

Berry compote or your choice of compote *as desired*

METHOD

1. Prepare five 120-ml ramekins. Prepare 5 pieces of clean gauze larger than the ramekins so there will be sufficient overhang to cover the filled ramekins. Soak gauze in water.

2. Combine fromage blanc, lemon zest, 5 g sweetener and Cointreau in a heatproof bowl set over a pot of simmering water. When fromage blanc is softened and sweetener is dissolved, set over a bowl of iced water to cool.

3. In a bowl, whisk double cream until stiff peaks form.

4. In another bowl, whisk egg white until foamy. Add 5 g sweetener and continue to whisk well.

5. Combine cream with egg white mixture.

6. Add egg mixture to fromage blanc mixture and mix well. Transfer to a piping bag (without a nozzle).

7. Wring dry the soaked gauze and line ramekins.

8. Pipe mixture equally into ramekins, taking care not to induce air as you pipe. Cover ramekins with overhanging gauze. Place a weight, such as another ramekin, over each ramekin. Leave in the refrigerator overnight. Serve with berry compote or a fruit compote of your choice.

CHOCOLATE MOUSSE
ショコラムース

Makes 5 servings

The hazelnut dacquoise and unsweetened chocolate are the ultimate combination in this chocolate mousse. Pipe plenty of whipping cream over and you'll be awed by how smooth the mousse is.

INGREDIENTS

Hazelnut Dacquoise

Egg yolks *2*

Natural sweetener granules *9 g + 9 g*

Egg whites *2*

Hazelnut meal *55 g*

Cornflour *3 g*

Desiccated coconut *as needed*

Chocolate Mousse

Unsweetened chocolate *50 g*

Cold-pressed sesame oil *20 g*

Egg yolks *2*

Natural sweetener granules *20 g*

Whipping cream (35%)
50 ml + 125 ml

Gelatine sheet *5 g, soaked in iced water and drained before using*

Decoration

Whipping cream (35%) *150 ml*

Mint *a few sprigs*

METHOD

1. Preheat oven to 200°C. Prepare five 6-cm wide ramekins and line a baking tray.

2. Prepare hazelnut dacquoise. Place egg yolks and 9 g sweetener in a bowl and mix with a whisk.

3. In another bowl, whisk egg whites well. Add 9 g sweetener and mix well.

4. Combine egg yolk and egg white mixtures using a rubber spatula and mix well. Sift in hazelnut meal and cornflour and stir to combine.

5. Transfer to a piping bag fitted with a 9-mm nozzle and pipe five 6-cm flat rounds on prepared tray (see photo). Sprinkle rounds with desiccated coconut.

6. Bake for 10–13 minutes. Remove from the oven and leave to cool. Trim dacquoise to fit ramekins.

7. Prepare chocolate mousse. Heat unsweetened chocolate and sesame oil in a heatproof bowl set over a pot of simmering water until mixture is smooth. Remove from heat.

8. Whisk egg yolks and sweetener in a bowl until well blended.

9. Heat 50 ml whipping cream in a saucepan over medium heat until lukewarm (about body temperature). Add whipping cream gradually to egg yolk mixture. Whisk and mix well.

10. Transfer mixture to a saucepan and warm over low heat to 80–85°C, stirring continuously using a rubber spatula.

11. Remove from heat. Add gelatine and mix well until dissolved.

12. Add mixture gradually to unsweetened chocolate mixture. Mix quickly using the rubber spatula.

13. In another bowl, whisk 125 ml whipping cream until soft peaks form. Add to chocolate mixture and mix well using a rubber spatula. Transfer to a piping bag.

14. To assemble chocolate mousse, line bottom of each ramekin with a hazelnut dacquoise and pipe in chocolate mousse.

15. Prepare decoration. Whisk whipping cream until stiff peaks form. Transfer to a piping bag with a nozzle of your choice and pipe cream onto chocolate mousse to decorate. Garnish with sprigs of mint. Refrigerate to chill before serving.

The hazelnut dacquoise and unsweetened chocolate are the ultimate combination in this chocolate mousse. You'll be awed by how smooth the mousse is.

SESAME BLANCMANGE
ごまのブラマンジェ

Makes 4 servings

I have used sesame seeds instead of the usual almonds for this blancmange. The fragrance of the white sesame paste makes this dessert simply delightful.

INGREDIENTS

White sesame paste *120 g*

Milk *14 ml*

Whipping cream (35%) *200 ml*

Natural sweetener granules *12 g*

Gelatine sheet *5 g, soaked in iced water and drained before using*

Decoration

Whipping cream (35%) *50 ml*

White sesame seeds *a little*

METHOD

1. Prepare four 200-ml serving glasses.

2. Combine white sesame paste, milk, whipping cream and sweetener in a pot and heat over medium heat until mixture is about to come to a boil.

3. Turn off the heat, add gelatine and mix well until dissolved.

4. Transfer mixture to a bowl or a large measuring cup, set over a bowl of iced water to cool.

5. Pour mixture equally into serving glasses and refrigerate to set.

6. Whisk whipping cream until stiff peaks form and pipe or spoon into glasses. Sprinkle with white sesame seeds.

NOTE
Japanese white sesame paste is made from roasted white sesame seeds. If you cannot find white sesame paste, roast 120 g white sesame seeds well and grind into a paste.

SUGAR CONTENT

Hisae's Recipe

2.07 g
per serving

20.82 g
per serving

Typical Recipe

TEA VERRINES
紅茶のヴェリーヌ

Makes 4 servings

Tea becomes cloudy when gelatine is added. Thus, I've used agar to retain the beautiful amber tea colour. In addition to the fragrance of the tea jelly, you can enjoy the milky flavour and silky texture of this sophisticated dessert.

INGREDIENTS

Mint leaves *a few sprigs*

Tea Agar

Water *100 ml*

Earl Grey tea leaves *8 g, placed in a tea bag*

Agar powder *2 g*

Natural sweetener granules *10 g*

Tea Mousse

Egg yolks *2*

Natural sweetener granules *10 g*

Whipping cream (35%)
200 ml + 100 ml

Earl Grey tea leaves *15 g*

Gelatine sheet *4 g, soaked in iced water and drained before using*

Jelly

Earl Grey tea leaves *3 g, placed in a tea bag*

Natural sweetener granules *5 g*

Lemon juice *5 ml*

Water *100 ml*

Gelatine sheet *3 g, soaked in iced water and drained before using*

METHOD

1. Prepare four 140-ml serving glasses.

2. Prepare tea agar. Heat water in a saucepan over medium heat. When water comes to a boil, add tea leaves and turn off the heat. Steep for about 10 minutes with the lid on.

3. Remove tea leaves and add agar powder. Heat mixture over low heat until it comes to a boil. Turn off the heat, add sweetener and stir to dissolve. Set aside to cool.

4. Transfer tea agar mixture to a tray or container and refrigerate to set. When tea agar has set, cut into 1-cm cubes.

5. Prepare tea mousse. Place egg yolks and sweetener in a bowl and beat with a whisk until well mixed.

6. Heat 200 ml whipping cream and tea leaves in a saucepan over medium heat until lukewarm (about body temperature). Add gradually to egg yolk mixture while whisking.

7. Transfer mixture back to the saucepan and warm over low heat to 80-85°C, stirring continuously using a rubber spatula.

8. Remove from heat. Add gelatine and mix well until dissolved. Transfer mixture to a bowl set over a bowl of iced water to cool until it is cooler than room temperature.

9. Whisk 100 ml whipping cream until soft peaks form and mix with gelatine mixture.

10. Pour tea mousse equally into serving glasses and refrigerate to set.

11. Prepare jelly. Heat tea leaves, sweetener, lemon juice and water in a saucepan over medium heat. When mixture comes to a boil, turn off the heat. Add gelatine and mix well until dissolved. Strain mixture and set over a bowl of iced water until it is cooler than room temperature.

12. Pour jelly equally into serving glasses. Add tea agar cubes to the jelly layer. Refrigerate to set jelly. Decorate with sprigs of mint.

PANNA COTTA
パンナコッタ

Makes 4 servings

> The sweetness of coconut and passion fruit gives this panna cotta a tropical feel. The passion fruit purée may be a little high in sugar, but I have kept the amount to a minimum while ensuring that the dessert is just as delightful.

INGREDIENTS

Milk *160 ml*

Whipping cream (35%) *300 ml*

Natural sweetener granules *35 g*

Gelatine sheet *8 g, soaked in iced water and drained before using*

Desiccated coconut *50 g*

Rum *8 ml*

Passion Fruit Jelly

Sugar-free passion fruit purée *50 g*

Natural sweetener granules *20 g*

Water *100 ml*

Gelatine sheet *4 g, soaked in iced water and drained before using*

METHOD

1. Prepare four 200-ml serving glasses.

2. Prepare panna cotta. Heat milk, whipping cream and sweetener in a saucepan over medium heat. When mixture comes to a boil, turn off the heat. Add gelatine and desiccated coconut, mix quickly. Steep for about 10 minutes with the lid on.

3. Strain mixture into a bowl and set over a bowl of iced water to cool. When mixture is cool, add rum and mix well.

4. Pour mixture equally into serving glasses and refrigerate to set.

5. Prepare passion fruit jelly. Heat passion fruit purée, sweetener and water in a saucepan over medium heat. When mixture comes to a boil, turn off the heat. Add gelatine and mix well until dissolved.

6. Strain mixture into a bowl and set over a bowl of iced water to cool.

7. Pour jelly equally into serving glasses and refrigerate to set.

VANILLA ICE CREAM
バニラアイスクリーム

Makes about 390 g ice cream

Just combine crème anglaise and double cream, then freeze it. This is as simple as it gets.

INGREDIENTS

Egg yolks 3

Natural sweetener granules 30 g

Salt a pinch

Whipping cream (35%) 250 ml

Vanilla seeds a small amount

Lemon juice 5 ml

Rum 2 ml

Double cream (42%) 80 ml

METHOD

1. Place egg yolks, sweetener and salt in a bowl and beat with a whisk until well mixed.

2. Heat whipping cream and vanilla seeds in a saucepan over medium heat until lukewarm (about body temperature). Add gradually to egg yolk mixture while whisking.

3. Transfer mixture to a saucepan and warm over low heat to 80–85°C, stirring continuously using a rubber spatula.

4. Remove from heat and strain into a bowl. When mixture is slightly cooled, set over a bowl of iced water to chill. Add lemon juice and rum to chilled mixture and mix well.

5. In a bowl, whisk double cream until stiff peaks form.

6. Add chilled mixture to double cream and mix well using a rubber spatula.

7. Pour into a freezer container and place in the freezer to set.

Fanciful
Desserts

RASPBERRY CHARLOTTE CAKE
シャルロット・オ・フランボワーズ

Makes one 15-cm cake, serves 6

Dacquoise biscuits are used for the base and sides of this charlotte cake. It is beautifully decorated with plenty of fruits, but raspberry is no doubt the star of this dessert. The raspberry mousse, made with home-made compote, is simply divine.

INGREDIENTS

Raspberry Compote

Raspberries *200 g*

Lemon juice *15 ml*

Liquid sweetener *35 g*

Dacquoise Cookie

Egg yolks *2*

Natural sweetener granules
9 g + 9 g

Egg whites *2*

Almond meal *55 g*

Cornflour *3 g*

Desiccated coconut *as needed*

Raspberry Mousse

Egg whites *2*

Natural sweetener granules *14 g*

Water *58 ml*

Gelatine sheet *5 g, soaked in iced water and drained before using*

Raspberry compote *100 g (recipe below)*

Whipping cream (35%) *100 ml*

Decoration

Fresh fruits of your choice
as desired

METHOD

1. Preheat oven to 200°C. Prepare a 15-cm cake ring.

2. Cut a piece of baking paper to fit a baking tray and draw a 15-cm circle at its centre. Draw two 35 x 6-cm rectangles on the remaining space. Line baking tray with baking paper.

3. Prepare raspberry compote. Heat raspberries, lemon juice and sweetener in a saucepan over medium heat until mixture is thick and sticky. Remove from heat and leave to cool.

4. Prepare dacquoise cookie. In a bowl, beat egg yolks until pale. Mix in 9 g sweetener. In another bowl, whisk egg whites until stiff peaks form. Mix in 9 g sweetener.

5. Combine egg yolk mixture and meringue and mix with a rubber spatula. Sift in almond meal and cornflour and mix very quickly. Transfer batter to a piping bag fitted with a 9-mm nozzle.

6. Pipe batter into a round spiral shape using the outline of the circle as a guide.

7. Pipe batter into 6-cm strips side by side on top of the rectangles. Continue to pipe any excess batter into strips. Sprinkle desiccated coconut over piped batter.

8. Bake for about 10 minutes. Remove from the oven and leave to cool on a wire rack.

9. Prepare raspberry mousse. Whisk egg whites with a hand-held mixer until foamy. Heat sweetener and water in a saucepan until mixture comes to a boil. Add boiled mixture gradually to egg whites while stirring. Continue stirring until mixture is cool.

10. Combine gelatine and 100 g raspberry compote in a heatproof bowl set over a pot of simmering water. Heat until gelatine is dissolved.

11. Combine egg white mixture and raspberry mixture and mix using a whisk.

12. In another bowl, whisk whipping cream until soft (see photo). Add to raspberry mixture and mix well.

13. Line the sides of the cake ring with rectangular dacquoise cookies and trim any excess. Place the round dacquoise cookie at the base.

14. Pour raspberry mousse over base and place in the freezer for 20-30 minutes to set. Decorate with fresh fruits of your choice before serving.

Dacquoise biscuits are used for the base and sides of this charlotte cake, but raspberry is no doubt the star of this dessert. The raspberry mousse, made with home-made compote, is simply divine.

OPERA CAKE
オペラ

Makes one 20 x 15-cm cake, serves 12

An established pâtisserie in Paris created this dessert inspired by the image of opera seats. The optimum thickness of each layer in the opera cake is 5 mm. This delicate cake is worth all the effort.

INGREDIENTS

Joconde Sponge

Unsalted butter *20 g*

Almond meal *100 g*

Natural sweetener granules *45 g*

Cornflour *5 g*

Eggs *3*

Egg whites *4*

Coffee Syrup

Coffee beans *30 g, ground*

Water *250 ml + 60 ml*

Liquid sweetener *35 g*

Rum *30 ml*

Ganache

Unsweetened chocolate *50 g*

Natural sweetener granules *20 g*

Whipping cream (35%) *70 ml*

Cold-pressed sesame oil *10 g*

Coffee Buttercream

Coffee beans *20 g, ground*

Water *50 ml*

Egg yolks *3*

Natural sweetener granules *10 g*

Whipping cream (35%) *110 ml*

Unsalted butter *160 g, at room temperature*

Chocolate Glaze

Couverture chocolate (unsweetened) *150 g*

Cold-pressed sesame oil *23 g*

Scan this QR code to watch a video tutorial on assembling Opera Cake.

19

21

METHOD

1. Preheat oven to 210°C. Line a 40 x 30-cm baking tray.

2. Prepare joconde sponge. Melt butter in a heatproof bowl set over a pot of simmering water. Set aside.

3. Combine almond meal, sweetener, cornflour and eggs in a heatproof bowl set over a pot of simmering water and whisk with a hand-held mixer until pale. Remove from heat.

4. In another bowl, whisk egg whites well.

5. Add egg whites to almond meal mixture and mix using a rubber spatula. Mix in melted butter.

6. Pour batter into prepared baking tray and spread evenly. Bake for about 13 minutes. Remove from the oven and leave to cool.

7. Prepare coffee syrup. Heat ground coffee beans and 250 ml water in a saucepan. When mixture comes to a boil, turn off the heat and leave to steep for about 5 minutes with the lid on. Strain coffee.

8. Mix sweetener, rum and 60 ml water in a bowl. Add coffee and mix well. Set aside.

9. Prepare ganache. Combine all ganache ingredients in a heatproof bowl and set over a pot of simmering water until mixture is smooth.

10. Remove from heat and blend mixture using a hand-held blender until emulsified.

11. Prepare coffee buttercream. Heat ground coffee beans and water in a saucepan. When mixture comes to a boil, turn off the heat and leave to steep for about 5 minutes with the lid on. Strain coffee and leave to cool.

12. In a bowl, whisk egg yolks and sweetener until well mixed.

13. Heat whipping cream in a saucepan over medium heat until lukewarm (about body temperature). Add gradually to egg yolk mixture while whisking.

14. Transfer mixture to a saucepan and warm over low heat to 80–85°C, stirring continuously using a rubber spatula. Turn off the heat and set over a bowl of iced water to chill. Add coffee and mix well.

15. In a bowl, beat butter with a hand-held mixer until fluffy. Add coffee mixture in a few additions and mix well each time. If the mixture separates, continue whisking until emulsified.

16. Divide buttercream into 3 portions: 100 g, 100 g and 50 g.

17. Assemble cake. Cut joconde sponge into 4 equal rectangles. Pour coffee syrup onto a tray and dip sponge cake into syrup one by one.

18. Place a sponge cake on a cake board or tray. Transfer 100 g buttercream to a piping bag fitted with a flat nozzle and pipe onto cake.

19. Place another sponge cake on top and build cake up with a layer of ganache, then sponge, 100 g buttercream, sponge and 50 g buttercream. This forms 8 layers, with each layer about 5 mm in height. Whenever you add a sponge layer, cover it with a piece of baking paper and press on it gently with the base of a tray before proceeding with the next layer. Place in the freezer to set.

20. Prepare chocolate glaze. Heat couverture chocolate and sesame oil in a heatproof bowl set over a pot of simmering water until mixture is smooth. Let glaze cool to room temperature.

21. Remove cake from the freezer. Over the centre of the cake, pour chocolate glaze and spread with a palette knife, moving it horizontally until the entire surface is evenly coated. Leave for a while to set. Remove the excess edges and slice to serve.

An established pâtisserie in Paris created this dessert inspired by the image of opera seats. This delicate cake is worth all the effort.

PARIS-BREST
パリブレスト

Makes one 12-cm pastry, serves 6

A dessert with a nutty flavour, this choux pastry is piped to resemble a bicycle wheel. This is a recipe to try when you have mastered how to make choux pastry.

INGREDIENTS

Paris-Brest Pastry

Unsalted butter *50 g*

Milk *50 ml*

Water *50 ml*

Salt *2 g*

Rice flour *60 g*

Egg *2.5*

Sliced almonds *as desired*

Hazelnut Custard Cream

Milk *100 ml*

Whipping cream (35%) *100 ml*

Vanilla seeds *a small amount*

Egg yolks *2*

Natural sweetener granules *25 g*

Gelatine sheet *6 g, soaked in iced water and drained before using*

100% hazelnut paste *15 g*

Double cream (42%) *100 ml*

METHOD

1. Prepare Paris-Brest pastry. Using the ingredients listed, follow Steps 1-5 on page 40 to make choux pastry batter.

2. Transfer batter to a piping bag fitted with a star-shaped nozzle. Pipe batter to form 2 concentric circles 12 cm in diameter. Repeat to pipe another smaller circle on the concentric circles (see photo). Any excess batter can be piped to form more choux pastries for other recipes.

3. Scatter sliced almonds on piped batter. Place tray into preheated oven. Turn off the oven and let sit for 5 minutes. Do not open the oven door during this time.

4. Turn on the oven to 180°C and bake for 35 minutes. Remove and leave choux pastry to cool on a wire rack.

5. Prepare hazelnut custard cream. Using the ingredients listed, follow Steps 9–13 on page 41.

6. Add hazelnut paste to mixture and mix well using a whisk.

7. In another bowl, whisk double cream until stiff peaks form.

8. Add double cream gradually to hazelnut mixture, keeping an eye on the texture of the custard cream.

9. Assemble pastry. Slice Paris-Brest pastry about one-third from the top using a knife.

10. Transfer hazelnut custard cream to a piping bag fitted with a star-shaped nozzle. Pipe onto the bottom half of the pastry and sandwich with the top half. Slice to serve.

NOTE
If you cannot find 100% hazelnut paste, roast 15 g hazelnuts well and grind into a paste.

Scan this QR code to watch a video tutorial on piping Paris-Brest pastry.

JEWEL BONBONS
ボンボンビジュー

Makes about 280 g jelly

This is the perfect sweet that has zero calories and does not contain any sugar. With their pretty colours, these bonbons look like sparkling jewels. Have fun making them in various shapes and colours!

INGREDIENTS

Agar powder *4 g*

Water *200 ml*

Your choice of food colouring
*a very small amount
(about 0.05 g)*

Natural sweetener granules *85 g*

METHOD

1. Prepare a 9-cm cake ring. Stretch cling film over one side to form a base and attach it securely to the ring.

2. Heat agar powder, water and food colouring in a saucepan over low heat. Keep stirring until agar powder is dissolved. (If you are using agar sheets, soak them in water and squeeze dry before quickly adding to the saucepan just as food colouring and water mixture is about to come to a boil.)

3. Add sweetener and heat mixture over high heat to 102°C.

4. Turn off the heat and set over a bowl of iced water to cool. (Be careful not to let the mixture become too cold as it will solidify.) Pour mixture into the prepared cake ring.

5. Leave at room temperature to set. This will take more than an hour. It can also be placed in the refrigerator to set more quickly.

6. When jelly has set, remove from the cake ring and cut into small pieces.

7. Leave bonbons on a tray to dry at room temperature before serving.

NOTE
For Step 3, if you do not have a cooking thermometer, remove from heat when the mixture is simmering (see photo). Return to heat when the mixture is no longer bubbling. Do this 3 times.

If you are making this in the winter, leave bonbons overnight at room temperature. In the summer, dry bonbons with the help of a fan. Do not use hot air.

Scan this QR code to watch a video tutorial on heating the mixture for Jewel Bonbons.

ALMOND CHOCOLATE CAKE
チョコレートとアーモンドのケーキ

Makes ten 7 x 3-cm cakes, serves 10

The addition of almonds to the chocolate coating adds a fun, crunchy texture to this substantial chocolate cake.

INGREDIENTS

Cocoa Sponge Cake (page 82) *1*

Buttercream

Unsalted butter *120 g, at room temperature*

Vanilla seeds *a small amount*

Natural sweetener granules *30 g*

Water *20 ml*

Egg *1*

Syrup

Natural sweetener granules *10 g*

Water *15 ml*

Rum *3 ml*

Chocolate Almond Coating

Diced almonds *50 g*

Unsweetened chocolate *150 g*

Cold-pressed sesame oil *15 g*

METHOD

1. Prepare buttercream. Mix butter and vanilla seeds together and set aside.

2. Heat sweetener and water in a saucepan until mixture comes to a boil.

3. Place egg in a bowl and beat with a hand-held mixer. Add boiled mixture gradually and continue stirring until cooled.

4. Add butter mixture to egg mixture gradually and continue mixing.

5. Prepare syrup. Heat sweetener and water in a saucepan until mixture comes to a boil. Turn off the heat, add rum and mix well.

6. Assemble cake. Slice cocoa sponge cake into 2 equal rectangles.

7. Place a sponge cake on a cake board or tray and brush with syrup. Spread one-third of the buttercream evenly on top using a palette knife.

8. Brush the remaining syrup on both sides of the other sponge cake and place on top of buttercream layer. Spread a thin layer of the remaining buttercream on the top and sides of the entire cake. Place in the freezer to set.

9. Prepare chocolate almond coating. Roast diced almonds at 160°C for about 15 minutes.

10. Heat unsweetened chocolate and sesame oil in a heatproof bowl set over a pot of simmering water. Mix in diced almonds and remove from heat.

11. Remove cake from the freezer and cut into 10 slices. Pour coating over each slice and refrigerate to set.

NOTE
At Step 5, the mixture may separate. Don't worry and continue whisking until it emulsifies.

The ideal temperature for making the coating is 32°C. If the chocolate starts to harden, you can always warm it up to soften it again.

Weights and Measures

Quantities for this book are given in Metric and American (spoon and cup) measures. Standard spoon and cup measurements used are: 1 teaspoon = 5 ml, 1 tablespoon = 15 ml, 1 cup = 250 ml. All measures are level unless otherwise stated.

LIQUID AND VOLUME MEASURES

Metric	Imperial	American
5 ml	1/6 fl oz	1 teaspoon
10 ml	1/3 fl oz	1 dessertspoon
15 ml	1/2 fl oz	1 tablespoon
60 ml	2 fl oz	1/4 cup (4 tablespoons)
85 ml	2 1/2 fl oz	1/3 cup
90 ml	3 fl oz	3/8 cup (6 tablespoons)
125 ml	4 fl oz	1/2 cup
180 ml	6 fl oz	3/4 cup
250 ml	8 fl oz	1 cup
300 ml	10 fl oz (1/2 pint)	1 1/4 cups
375 ml	12 fl oz	1 1/2 cups
435 ml	14 fl oz	1 3/4 cups
500 ml	16 fl oz	2 cups
625 ml	20 fl oz (1 pint)	2 1/2 cups
750 ml	24 fl oz (1 1/5 pints)	3 cups
1 litre	32 fl oz (1 3/5 pints)	4 cups
1.25 litres	40 fl oz (2 pints)	5 cups
1.5 litres	48 fl oz (2 2/5 pints)	6 cups
2.5 litres	80 fl oz (4 pints)	10 cups

DRY MEASURES

Metric	Imperial
30 grams	1 ounce
45 grams	1 1/2 ounces
55 grams	2 ounces
70 grams	2 1/2 ounces
85 grams	3 ounces
100 grams	3 1/2 ounces
110 grams	4 ounces
125 grams	4 1/2 ounces
140 grams	5 ounces
280 grams	10 ounces
450 grams	16 ounces (1 pound)
500 grams	1 pound, 1 1/2 ounces
700 grams	1 1/2 pounds
800 grams	1 3/4 pounds
1 kilogram	2 pounds, 3 ounces
1.5 kilograms	3 pounds, 4 1/2 ounces
2 kilograms	4 pounds, 6 ounces

OVEN TEMPERATURE

Regulo	°C	°F	Gas
Very slow	120	250	1
Slow	150	300	2
Moderately slow	160	325	3
Moderate	180	350	4
Moderately hot	190/200	370/400	5/6
Hot	210/220	410/440	6/7
Very hot	230	450	8
Super hot	250/290	475/550	9/10

LENGTH

Metric	Imperial
0.5 cm	1/4 inch
1 cm	1/2 inch
1.5 cm	3/4 inch
2.5 cm	1 inch